FURNITURE FOR SMALL HOUSES

FURNITURE FOR SMALL HOUSES

PERCY A WELLS

CLASSIC EDITIONS

CONTENTS.

CHAP.   PAGE

I. INTRODUCTION   I

II. TABLES   5

The Gate Leg Table—Leaf and Extending Tables—Round and Elliptic
Tops—The "Kitchen" and Dining Tables—Types of Construction—
Small Tables.

III. DRESSERS AND SIDEBOARDS   II

The Fixed Dresser—Open Shelves—Glass Doors—The Dwarf Dresser—
The Sideboard—Clock Cases—Coal Boxes.

IV. CHAIRS   19

The Windsor and Stick Back Chairs—Stuff-over and Loose Seats—
Wooden Seats and Loose Cushions—The Settee, the Couch, and the
Settle.

V. BEDROOM FURNITURE   23

Bedsteads—Wardrobes—Washstands—Combing.

VI BEDROOM FURNITURE (continued)   29

Chests of Drawers—Toilet Mirrors—Towel Horses and Rails.

VII. MISCELLANEOUS FURNITURE   33

Book Cases—China Cabinets—Hat Stands—Whatnots.

LIST OF PLATES AND TEXT ILLUSTRATIONS.

A.

Arm-chairs, XXV, XXIX.

B.

Bedrooms, large, I.
— small, III.
Bedroom furniture, I, III.
Bedsteads, XL, XLV.
Book cases, XV, LVI.
— racks, LV, LVI.
Button fastenings, fig. 7.

C.

Chairs, V, XVI, XXIV, XXV, XXVI, XX-
    VIII, XXX, XXXV, XLVIII, LIV.
Chesterfields, XXVII.
Chests, dressing, XXXIV, XXXV, L.
— of drawers, XLVII.
— painted, XXXIV, XXXV.
China shelves, XXVI, LV.
— cupboards, LIV, LVI.
Clock cases, figs. 5, 6.
Coal scuttle, fig. 2.
Coat rack, fig. 11.
Combing, XLVI, fig. 9.
Corner cupboards, LVII, fig. 8.
Couch, XXVII.
Cupboards, XVII, XXXVI, figs. 2, 8.
Cupboard chests, XVII, L.

D.

Designs, XXVIII, XXIX, LII.
Dressers, dwarf, XV, XIX, XX.
— glass doors, XIX.
— open, frontispiece, XVIII.
— small, XIV, XX, XXI.
Dressing chests, XXXIV, XXXV, L.

F.

Frames, mirror, LII.

H.

Hall seat, XXIV.
Hat stand, LIII.
Hat rack, fig. 11.

L.

Living room, II.
Log box, fig. 4.
Loose seat, XVI.

M.

Mahogany, XVI, XXIII.
Mirrors, XVII, LII.

O.

Oak, I, XVI, XXII, XXIV, LIII.

P.

Painted work, III.
Paper Rack, LVI.
Parlour, XXVI.
Plate cupboard, fig. 2.

S.

Settee, XXVII.
Settle, XXVII.
Shelves, XXVI.
Sideboards, XVI, XXII, XXIII.
Splash curtains, XXXIV.

T.

Tables, bedside, VIII, XXXIV.
— dining, fig. 1.

LIST OF PLATES AND TEXT ILLUSTRATIONS

Tables, dressing, XXXIV, XLVIII.
— extension, VI, IX, XI.
— flap, XIII.
— framed up, IV, X.
— gate leg, IV, XIII.
— kitchen, V, X.
— large, I, IV.
— living room, VI, VII.
— toilet, XLVIII, LI.
— trestle, XII.
— side, VIII.
— small, VI, VIII.
Toilet glasses, LII.
Towel horses, XLVII, XLIX.
— rails, XLIX, fig. 10.

U.

Umbrella stand, LIII.

W.

Wall flaps, XIII.
Wardrobes, XXXI, XXXII, XXXIII, XXXVIII, XXXIX, XLI.
Wardrobes, double doors, XXXIII, XXXIX.
Wardrobes, framed up, XXXI, XLIV.
— painted, XXXII, XXXIII.
— small, XXXVIII, XLIII.
— with drawers, XLII.
Washstands, corner, XXXV, XXXVI.
— lino top, XXXIV, XXXVII.
— painted, XXXIII, XXXVII.
— tambour front, XXXIV.
Whatnots, XXVI, LV.

FURNITURE FOR SMALL HOUSES.

I. INTRODUCTION.

THE title of this book is intended to include all the smaller types of houses in town or country, whether they be known by the name of villa or cottage. The designs have been prepared in response to hundreds of applications—many from overseas—for assistance in producing pleasant and inexpensive furniture.

It is still happily possible to step into a seventeenth century living room in a wayside cottage or farm-house which has not yet felt the modern touch in furnishing. The instant impression that one gets is of a simple dignity and homely restfulness. The gate-leg table, the dresser, the sturdy chairs, all seem so fit for their place and purpose. It would be absurd to claim that such furniture is altogether suitable for modern needs, but now that thousands of well-planned cottages are to be built it is reasonable to hope that something of the quiet dignity and fitness may be introduced into their furnishing. A well-known and large manufacturer of furniture has recently said that " the humblest home can be made pleasant at no greater expense than is incurred in making it ugly ". The designs contained in the following pages are an earnest attempt to prove that the claim made in that statement is both possible and practicable.

It is not claimed that the attempt exhausts the possibilities of design, construction, or finish in suitable furniture for small houses. There is a wide field for local craftsmanship and tradition to vary both form and the manner of making. The designs here shown are done more for experiment and suggestion. Some new ideas have been introduced in the making and finishing. There is no article which cannot be produced by modern methods, hand or machine. Ease in moving and cleaning, and a minimum of work in dusting—pressing needs of the housewife—have been duly considered. Non-essentials, such as cornices and pediments,

1

have been discarded, and the whole aim of the designer has been to suggest a type of furniture which is useful, pleasant to look at, and moderate in price. It is readily admitted that the great bulk of cheap furniture has been both flimsy and ugly. Little or no thought has been given to suitable proportions and dimensions for small rooms. The designers and manufacturers must not take all the blame for this, for the public have been too ready to demand a showy article with plenty of polish and plate glass rather than a really serviceable one. This is well illustrated by the type of sideboard or overmantel overloaded with ugly and useless details which add to the cost and mean so much labour to keep clean. On the other hand, if the public are to be educated in selection and taste, education can only come through the designers and makers who put the goods on the market, and the salesman who comes into personal contact with the purchaser. There is now a decided demand for brighter homes and better furniture, and there is no excuse that ugliness and flimsy work should be the commonly accepted features of cheap goods. Fitness for use, good proportions, and bright, pleasant colour will not cost any more than bad proportions and unpleasant colour. As a matter of fact they should cost less, for better proportions would mean a reduction in material, and good lines on the inevitable " apron " or " curtain " pieces could be cut quicker than the coarse, switchback, curves which are made to fit any job or position. Machine productions should make no difference to the right application of the above principles, and we have to get rid of the fallacy that machine-made articles must necessarily be unpleasant in form and repulsive to good taste. It is hoped that the general public will begin to realise some of these simple and practical principles, and to apply them when purchasing household goods. With a public asking for better things and knowing what they wanted there would be no doubt as to improvement in quality.

A complete set of the furniture illustrated has been made, with the consent of the Education Authorities of the London County Council, at the Shoreditch Technical Institute. The set comprised a more or less completed furnishing for a five-roomed cottage, including a living room, parlour, and three bedrooms. The articles in the largest bedroom (see Plate I) were made of birch and whitewood polished only. In the living room (Plate II), the chairs were made of birch and the other articles of whitewood and deal. These were stained a light brown and polished.

The sets in the smaller bedrooms were made of deal and painted (Plate III). The painting was done as an experiment. Hitherto, cheap bedroom furniture has either been stained to imitate mahogany or walnut or grained in a wretched attempt to make it look like oak or maple. Paint, as a medium for finish, offers many advantages. It is durable, easily applied, and it gives a wide field for variety in bright and pleasant colours. Above all there is no sham or imitation about it. Plain painting in one or two colours would be infinitely better than the ugly yellow oak graining. This graining is done with a steel comb, and in the two bedroom sets a similar process has been adopted in two colours of paint, for example, blue superimposed on green. The combing is done before the blue is dry, and the green shows through the combings. An almost limitless number of patterns can be done by the comb (see Plate XLVI), and it is obvious that there can also be a wide variety of colours. Paint has a great advantage over stain in that the cheaper woods, such as deal, and "seconds" or "thirds" in pine, which are not suitable for staining, are quite adequate for painted furniture. The cheap bedroom "suites" of satin-walnut, though ugly in design, would look more pleasant painted in good colours than polished in the ghastly yellow which has always been the recognised finish for them. Is it not time that the "trade" began to consider the need for a brighter and more honest finish for cheap goods? Here, at least, is a suggestion for anyone to carry beyond the experimental stage. The special construction for painted work will be described in detail when the actual making of the articles is under discussion in the chapters devoted to wardrobes, dressers, chest of drawers, etc., etc., but the designer disclaims any desire for finality in design, construction, or finish. It is agreed that cheap production can only be obtained by a large output, and that to a certain extent standardisation is inevitable. There is not so much to fear in this if local traditions are allowed for, and there is plenty of play and opportunity for variety in form and colour without adding to the cost or seriously interfering with standard methods of production.

The author is indebted to the Design and Industries Association [1] for much help and encouragement. This Association is composed of manufacturers, designers, and business men and women who are interested in the betterment of household goods. They maintain that these things

[1] 6 Queen Square, W.C. 1.

can be both "cheap and good," and are ready to encourage any effort in that direction. In pursuance of this policy the Association has taken a first-hand interest in this experimental furniture. The suggestion that paint would make a better and brighter finish for furniture was immediately taken up, and the Association obtained permission from the L.C.C. to carry out experiments at the Brixton School of Building. The two painted bedroom sets are a result of these experiments in combed paint. Many of the other designs in the book could be treated in a similar manner. The Association secured the loan of the furniture for exhibition purposes, and arrangements are being made with firms to put the articles on the market.

The author gratefully acknowledges the generous co-operation of *the Principal (S. Hicks, Esq.), Miss H. J. Plowright, and members of* the Staff at the Shoreditch Technical Institute.

Plate I

A Bedroom with a Complete Set of Furniture

Plate II

Corner of a Living Room

Plate III

A Small Bedroom with Painted Furniture

II. TABLES.

The "Gate-Leg" Table—Leaf and Extending Tables—Round and Elliptic Tops—The "Kitchen" and Dining Table—Types of Construction —Small Tables.

FOR nearly three hundred years the old-time "Gate Leg" has held its own as a popular and useful type for the cottage or the modern dining-room. It has been made in all sizes and shapes : round, elliptical, square, oblong, and octagonal. The legs have been turned, twisted, and moulded, chamfered or left quite plain and square. Its outstanding virtue over other types is the ease by which it can be changed from its full size to nearly half, and again to a still smaller dimension. No other type of table is so easily packed away when the floor of the room is required. It has also one other quality which flap tables as a rule do not possess—namely—it cannot be tipped over, for the flaps have a downright support. The one objection to the gate table is that it has too many legs which are said to get in the way of the sitter. This objection applies chiefly to the end legs of the centre frame, but the hindrance is rather in the bottom rail which prevents the feet being put under the table. The photograph in Plate IV clearly shows this objection. These low under-rails were originally used to rest the feet upon when floors were of stone or were strewn with rushes. As these foot rails are not necessary now there is good reason for changing the construction of the table in such a way as to remove the obstruction to comfortable sitting. The design for the gate table on Plate XIII shows the rail set back from the legs, and as the top projects a good six inches there should be room for knees and feet, provided the table legs are far enough apart to take them. The setting back of the rails also involve some slight alterations in fixing the gate. The table in Plate IV shows the old form of construction where the rails are halved out to take the shutting

(5)

leg, which, when closed, is flush with the outside legs. In the new design the short rail which supports the gate is halved into the long rail and projects beyond it to take the pin upon which the gate swings. The top pin swings from a hole under the table top or from a piece screwed on to the rail. The top of the table must project far enough to take the thickness of the leg and leave a clearance for the flap to fall at right angles. In adopting this method there is no need for the halving of either the leg or the long rail. The plan of the top of this table is round, but as a rule an elliptical form is acknowledged to be the best and most serviceable shape. The table in Plate IV shows an oblong with round ends. The dimensions are 5 ft. by 2 ft. 10 in. and the top and framing were made of white deal, which necessitated a wide clamp on the flaps.

In its origin the "Gate Leg" was essentially a kitchen or "living" room table, associated with the cottage or farm-house. Though extremely useful in the way already described, it is costly to construct owing to the double number of legs. This fact alone may explain the reason for its decreasing use in the smaller homes. The ordinary kitchen table made of deal, with a drawer at one end, has long since taken its place. On the same Plate (XIII) as the gate table are two diagrams and details of useful table flaps fixed to the wall. The larger one is supported by two braced brackets fixed to a wall batten. Such flaps are extremely useful for temporary purposes and take up but little room when closed.

The well-known types of common kitchen tables are in two forms of construction. One, called the "Pembroke," with turned legs, has a flap to each side which is supported on brackets. The centre part is narrow, and consequently when the flaps are up the table is easily tipped over. The second type is usually made of white deal. The legs are tapered on the inside or turned ; there is a drawer at one end, and the top is generally made of three-quarter inch stuff thicknessed up at the ends. In thousands of small houses it is the table at which all meals are taken, and there is no reason why its design should not be improved without increasing its cost. A turned leg increases the work of dusting, and it costs more than a plain taper. To thickness up a thin top takes time and material. The drawing on Plate X shows an attempt to make this common table a little more interesting and pleasant in form.

The top—not thicknessed up—is rounded on the ends. The legs are tapered on the inside and a chamfer run down each corner and along the lower edge of the frame rail. In the drawer are two divisions (see plan) which can be removed if required, but it is reasonable to suppose that any housewife would welcome such a simple arrangement as a knife box. With these new details and good proportions this table, see Plate V, would not be so easily stamped as "common," or only good enough for the kitchen. On Plates IV and X an alternative design is given. The legs are square with chamfered edges and under rails are introduced. The design is suitable for a large table five or six feet long. Drawers could be added if desired, but it should be noted that they always add considerably to the cost. In all the table designs the tenons are shown as being pinned through the leg. This precaution increases the strength of the frame and is particularly desirable in a table which is subject to a good deal of moving. Details of moulded edges and chamfered or rounded legs are given with the designs.

On Plate VIII are three small tables. They can be made in hard or soft wood. A is suitable for a small parlour as a tea or card table. B is suggested as most useful as a bedside table. C would serve as a side table for writing or for extra things at meal times. The flap is supported by two " thumb " brackets which work on a centre and are pulled out as shown. Two of such small tables are given in Plate VI.

Extending tables are made in various forms, the best-known types being the " telescope " or " tray frame," methods which are used in the heavier and larger kind of dining tables. Another method is based on the Elizabethan "shovel-board" or "drawinge" table, but all these methods are expensive. On Plate IX a form of extension is shown which is applied to a plain table. Two sliders pull out at each end and support a leaf. By a simple arrangement of rails the leaves can be slipped underneath the top. The section shows the leaves in position when packed away. To keep the leaves flat a dovetail key can be run through on the under side or they can be clamped. A short dowel to drop into each slider will keep the leaves in position. One leaf in use will increase the table room for two people. It is quite impossible to have a drawer in this table, although a leaf extension can be applied to a table with a drawer which can be used to support the leaf, but the leaves cannot be packed away underneath when not in use. The safest principle is to accept the limits of construction and confine them to one or the other, the leaves without a drawer, or vice versa. The extension table— closed, is shown in Plate VI.

On Plate XI another form of leaf extension is shown. The method is similar to the last named, but the leaves are applied to the sides of the table instead of the ends, an arrangement which prevents the leaves being packed away as in the former design. A detail shows the section of the sliders held in position by a thin metal slip. This

Fig. 1.—An Oak Dining Table.

table without the leaves would be quite strong and serviceable. The top hangs over at the ends a sufficient length to ensure a comfortable sitting and the under rail should be high enough to allow for it. A photograph of the table made in oak without leaves is given in Fig. 1.

The " trestle " type of table is illustrated in Plate XII. Made in oak, deal, or birch it is quite strong, but drawers cannot be fitted to it. The small table in the lower corner of the page is very simple in construction, the struts taking the place of long side rails.

A framed-up table where the legs are tenoned into a foot piece is shown in Plate VII. The top is rounded on the ends, and although a little more costly to produce, this type makes a good centre table for a living room. This table, and the one with extension leaves, are shown in Plate VI.

Plate IV

A Large Table for a Living Room

A "Gate-Leg" Table made in White Deal

Plate V

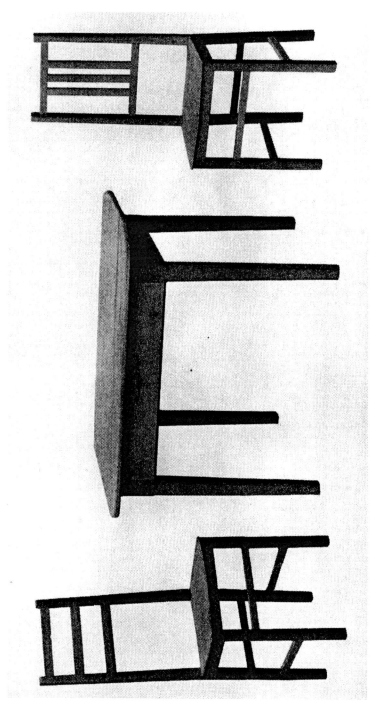

"Kitchen" Table and Two Chairs

Plate VI

LIVING ROOM TABLE   EXTENSION TABLE, CLOSED

TWO SMALL TABLES

PLATE VII

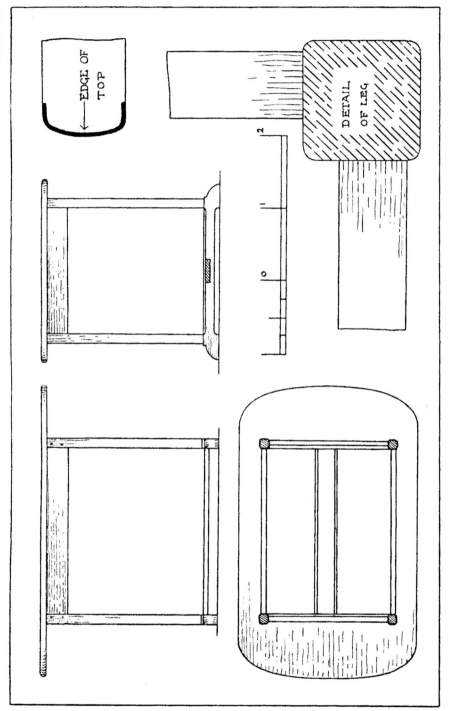

EDGE OF TOP

DETAIL OF LEG

A LIVING ROOM TABLE

Plate VIII

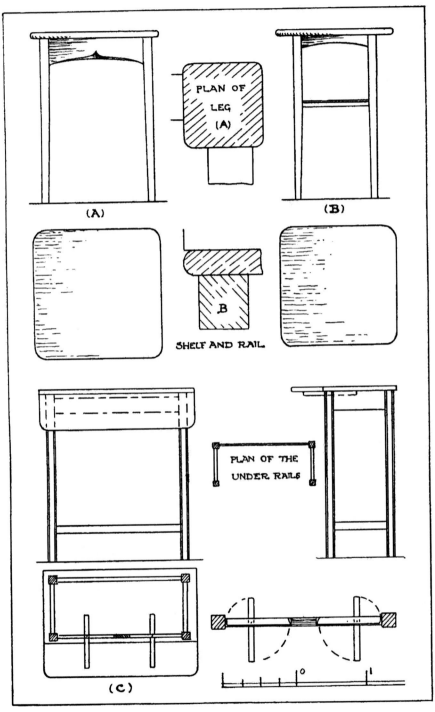

PLAN OF
LEG
(A)

(A)

(B)

B

SHELF AND RAIL

PLAN OF THE
UNDER RAILS

(C)

(1) Small Tables   (2) A Side Table with Flap

PLATE IX

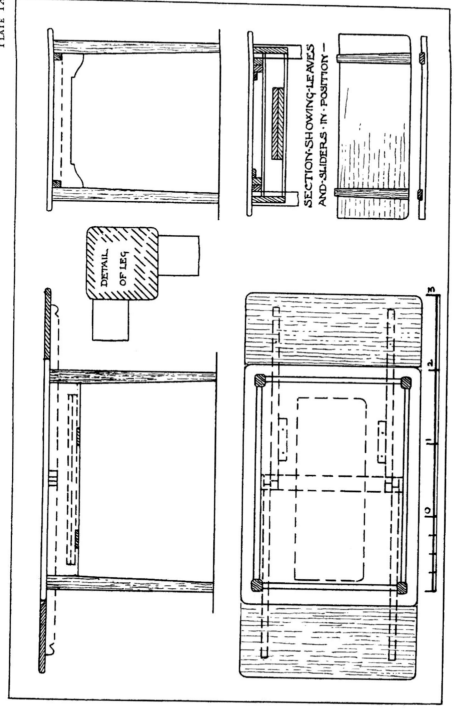

SECTION·SHOWING·LEAVES AND·SLIDERS·IN·POSITION

DETAIL OF LEG

A TABLE WITH END-LEAF EXTENSION

PLATE X

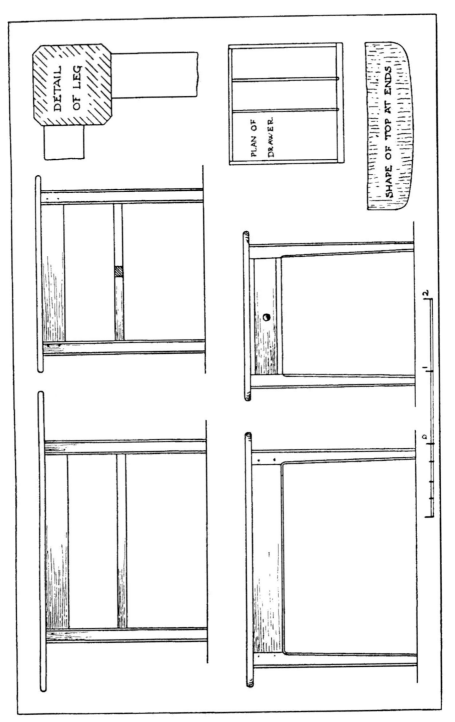

DETAIL OF LEG

PLAN OF DRAWER

SHAPE OF TOP AT ENDS

"KITCHEN" TABLES

Plate XI

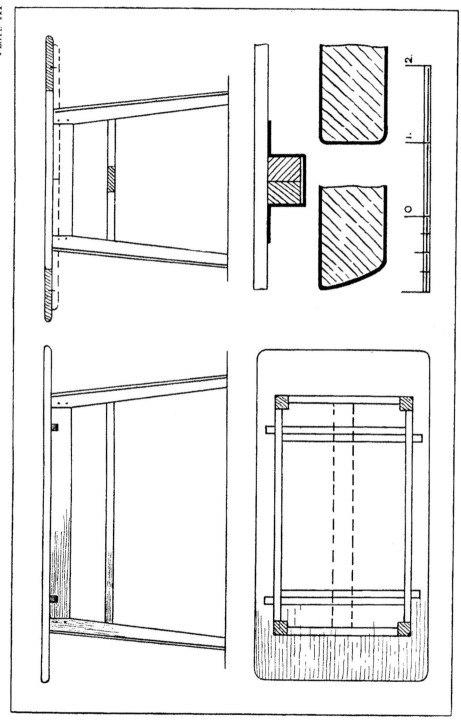

A Table with Side-Leaf Extension

PLATE XII

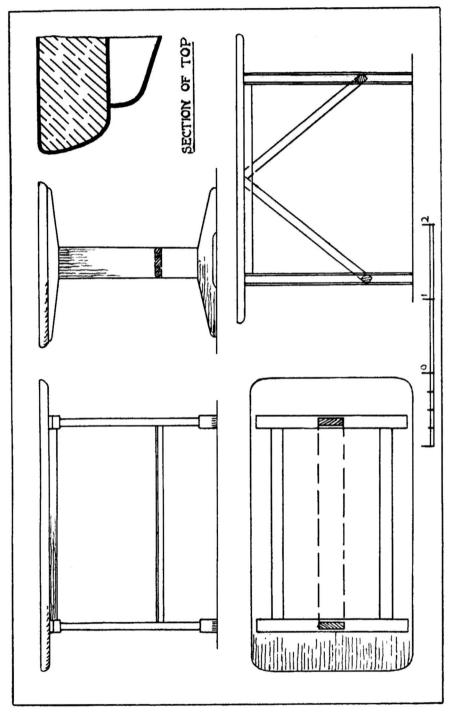

SECTION OF TOP

"TRESTLE" TABLES

Plate XIII

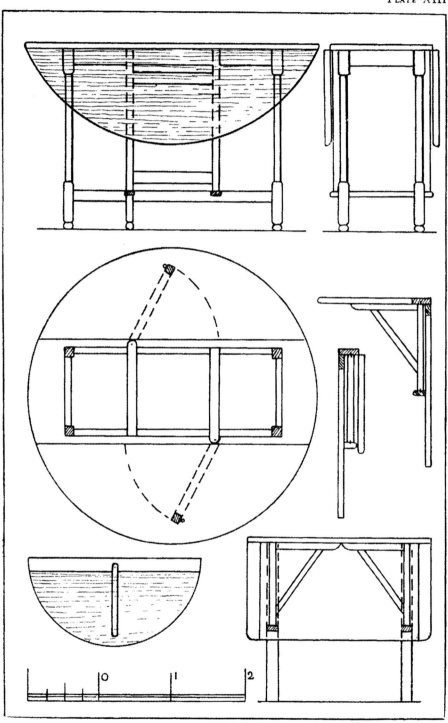

A Gate Table and Wall Flaps

III. DRESSERS AND SIDEBOARDS.

The Fixed Dresser—Open Shelves—Glass Doors—The Dwarf Dresser—The
Sideboard—Clock Cases—Coal Boxes.

In the designs for the new cottages it has been agreed that a large room
shall be provided which should serve the double purpose of kitchen and
living room. In the Report of the "Women's Housing Sub-Com-
mittee" it is recommended that a dresser with glass doors in the upper
part should be provided for this room. It may be taken for granted
that this dresser would be made a fixture and would also be similar in
design to the ordinary type found in kitchens. The above Report
suggests that there should be drawers and cupboards in the lower
part. The question of glass doors is open to criticism. In the first
place they would add very considerably to the cost of the dresser.
It can be safely assumed that the china on the shelves would be used
for at least three meals a day, and there would be very little time for
plates or dishes to get dusty. Glass doors would also mean more
work to keep them clean and some expense if the glass gets broken.

In such a case it were better to have wooden panels instead of
glass. The best ornament for a dresser is the china : jugs and cups
hanging on hooks and plates resting on shelves at the back, so that if
doors are to be added, the upper part, or carcase, must be made deeper
than on the usual dresser, whilst the shelves should be narrower to take
the jugs. There is one thing which should be duly considered before
an expensive dresser is fixed. In addition to any type of fixed dresser
it is more than probable that a bought cabinet or sideboard will form
part of the furniture of such a large living room. People will have
vases and ornaments and it is highly improbable that they will ever display
them on a "kitchen" dresser, whether closed or open. It is to meet
such a demand as this that designs for small sideboards of the dresser
type are provided in this chapter. It may also be stated that in

(11)

thousands of old small houses there is no dresser in the living room, and the occupants have to fall back on the modern cheap "chiffonier" or sideboard which may be anything but good or pleasant. In the frontispiece is a picture of a small open dresser, the details of which are given on Plate XVIII. This dresser is 3 ft. 6 ins. long. It stands up from the floor and the top is not too high to dust. The shelves can be easily reached, and the shelf in the bottom cupboard is shaped as shown on the plan so that tall jars or bottles can be placed in the cupboard. The ends are of $\frac{3}{4}$ in. stuff dowelled into posts, but they could of course be framed and panelled. The rails of the doors are chamfered on the inside edges, but as far as leaving no edge at all for dust to settle upon, a plain rounded surface is even better than a chamfer. The door panels are sunk with a slight hollow. The back of the top part is made of matched boarding which in a dresser of this kind is quite the most effective type of back to use. Wooden knobs are used for doors and drawers. The whole thing was made in white-wood, stained a light brown, waxed and set with a rubber polish.

The next dresser, on Plate XIX, is enclosed with doors. Glass can be used if desired. The carcases are constructed in a similar way to the last named. A third drawer has been added, and it is obvious that the cost has been considerably increased by the addition of the doors and the extra drawer. Although made in soft wood, the designs are quite suitable for oak or walnut. The small dresser at the bottom of the same page would be found most useful in a small room when upper shelves are not required. One advantage of having the cupboard above the drawers is that stooping is avoided as much as possible. The shelf at the bottom of the dresser could be used for boots.

On Plate XX is a design for a small dresser without drawers, but with a shelf at the back for china or books, and a full width shelf at the bottom. A detail of the door rail with a rounded edge in preference to a chamfer is shown to a large scale. A photograph of this dresser appears on Plate XIV.

Two designs for dwarf dressers are given on Plate XXI, and the top one is seen in Plate XV. The construction is simple and straight-forward, the carcase being fitted down on to a framed-up stool. The lower one has posts running right through and an under rail at the back and ends only.

It is difficult nowadays to define just where a dresser ends and a sideboard begins, for both are used for the same purpose, but taking a tier of shelves as defining a dresser, the design on Plate XXII can be safely described as a sideboard. It has been made in oak for which the design is most suitable. Drawers are omitted solely on the score of cost, but it would be quite easy to fit one inside if required. The

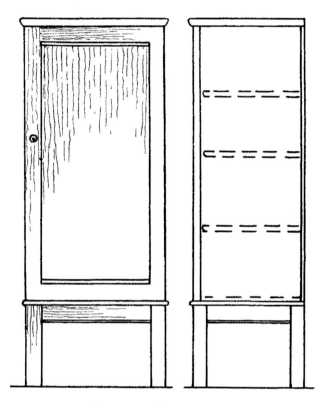

Fig. 2.—A Plate Cupboard.

chamfered finish to the post is given at A ; the section B shows the moulding run through the front division, whilst C and D give enlarged details of the bevelling on the back and the edge of the door. Plate XVI shows this little sideboard with a chair.

On Plate XXIII is a more costly design for a sideboard in mahogany. The tall cupboard in the centre has been arranged for bottles, and the shelves at the back are suitable for books or china. A is the cornice moulding, B the top, C section of door, and D the bevel under top. A photograph of a similar design with one chair is shown in Plate XVI.

In all these designs it has been the aim of the author to reduce sizes to a minimum and more in proportion to small rooms. Mouldings have been kept as simple as possible. Needless to say that the articles would be quite as useful without the little ornamentation which has been introduced, but utility, though first, is not the only thing to consider in furnishing a home.

For a scullery or kitchen a plate cupboard like that in Fig. 2 is often more handy and convenient than a larger dresser. It is just a box 3 ft. high and 18 ins. wide screwed on to a stool which is 1 ft. high. The end view shows the shelves. As a cupboard for odd things which cannot stand or hang on a dresser it is invaluable to the housewife.

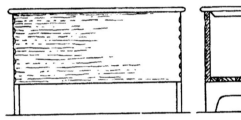

FIG. 3.—A Wooden Coal Box.

FIG. 4—A Log Box.

In the general view of the living room, Plate II, a wooden coal box is seen, of which Fig. 3 is a line drawing. It is a suggestion for a simpler and easier type of coal scuttle than the many which are now used. The change from metal to wood is suggested as being less noisy and more durable. The one in the photograph is made of $\frac{1}{2}$ in. birch and dovetailed together, but if it were well nailed and secured with metal corners it would be equally strong. The pieces underneath are shaped like rockers so that the box is easily tipped when the coal shovel is in use. For logs of wood a strong box which can be used as a seat is shown in Fig. 4. It is about 2 ft. long and 17 ins. high. The ends are cut out to receive the front and back which are strongly nailed and the edges are bevelled as shown. A brace screwed under the top should keep it flat.

In almost every cottage living room some piece of furniture in the nature of a chest of drawers is looked upon as absolutely essential to its furnishing. In many cases it is an old bureau which is a family heirloom, but where this is absent the general choice is for a chest of drawers, especially the well-known type where the plinth pulls out with the drawer. Many of these chests have been given in exchange for a good bureau. On Plate XVII there is a design for a cupboard chest which should answer all the purposes of the bureau or shoddy chest of drawers and even surpass them. It could be made in deal or whitewood and

Fig. 5.—Clock Cases.

painted, or in oak or birch and polished. It is 3 ft. 10 ins. high and 2 ft. 7 ins. wide. In the top is a cupboard with a fall-down flap. A narrow shelf runs round the ends and back of the cupboard space, leaving the whole height in the centre. Then come the drawers, and below them an open shelf for boots or such things as are needed every day. The construction can be similar to the painted chest of drawers, described in Chapter VI. There can be no doubt that failing a dresser or sideboard such a chest would be an untold blessing in a living room. A book rack on the top would add to its usefulness.

When will some enterprising "little master" take up the job of making simple but well-designed clock cases? When one looks in the clock shops how very few of the wooden clock cases are worth buying, to say nothing of the atrocious designs in black slate or pseudo marble. There should be a fortune for some one who can both design and finish cases to fit the standard sizes of clocks. To a cabinetmaker it should be an opportunity for using up small waste wood and veneer. In Fig. 5 are two out of forty cases which have been made at the Shoreditch

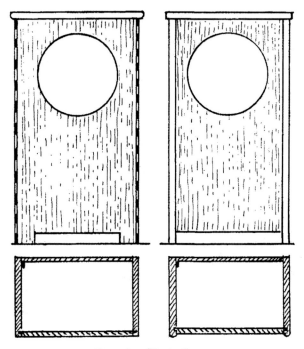

Fig. 6.—Clock Cases.

Institute. They were all of one size to take a pre-war 5s. 6d. American clock, but they all varied in colour and wood. In Fig. 6 are two even simpler designs. The cases are about 11 ins. high and 6 ins. wide, tongued and grooved together. They are easily decorated by a restrained use of a box or black line or narrow banding, but many of the odd pieces of veneer which are thrown away could be utilised. A hinged door at the back is necessary, and it can be readily seen that there is an endless variety in form, simple detail, and colour if the making of cases is seriously taken up.

In planning the new cottages there are one or two incidentals which should be considered, and particularly in regard to fixed cupboards in the recesses and the treatment of the shelf over the fireplace. Assuming a recess on each side of the chimney breast it would be unfortunate if the usual procedure were followed and cupboards fixed to fill the recess from the floor upwards. This at once decreases the floor space and causes endless inconvenience to the housewife who wants to use the cupboard, especially when her good husband has to move his chair for the door to be opened. The remedy for this is to raise the cupboards above chair height. On Plate XVII there is a diagram to illustrate this point. A fixed dresser and two such cupboards above a shelf, as are shown, should provide enough storage accommodation in a living room. The diagram also gives another suggestion for a fixed glass over the mantel shelf. People will have a mirror of some sort over the fireplace. In cottages it is the husband's toilet glass. If the architect does not fix one, his well-designed room will be spoiled by the common overmantel with its tiers of shelves, plate glass panels, and fretwork, which still has a strange fascination amongst the common furniture buyers.

PLATE XIV

A SMALL DRESSER WITHOUT DRAWERS

Plate XV

A Dwarf Dresser and Bookcase Cupboard

PLATE XVI

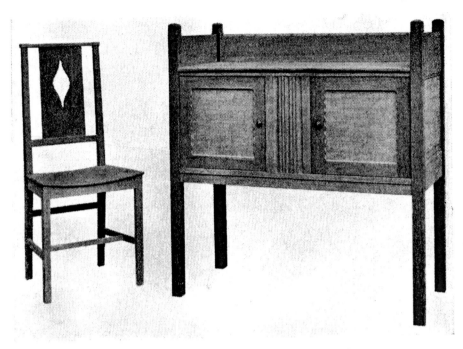

AN OAK SIDEBOARD AND CHAIR WITH WOODEN SEAT

A MAHOGANY SIDEBOARD AND CHAIR WITH LOOSE SEAT

Plate XVII

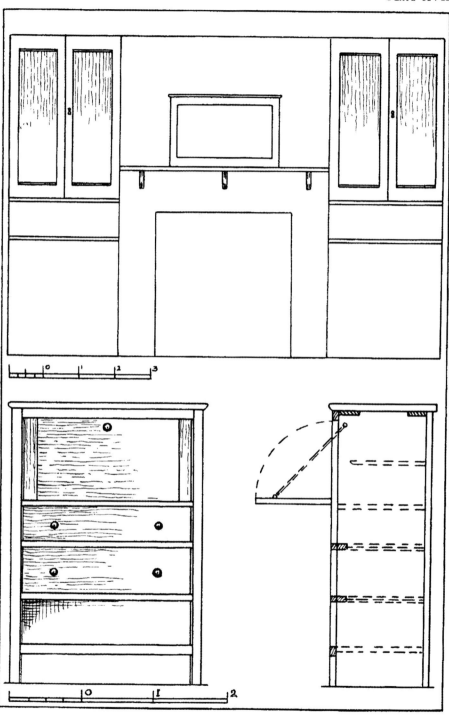

(1) Cupboards Fixed in Recesses (2) A Cupboard Chest for a Living Room

PLATE XVIII

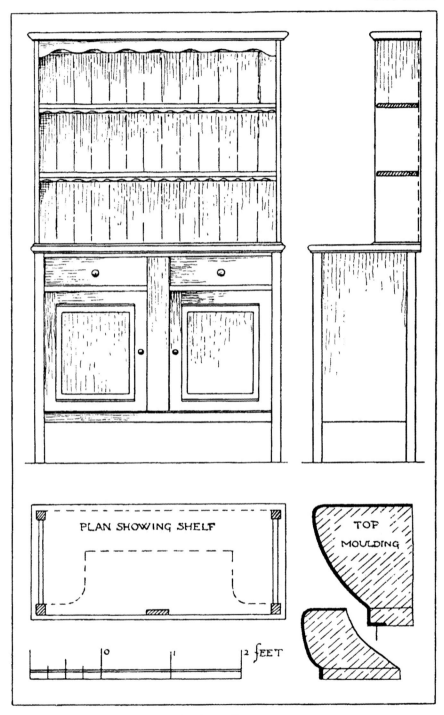

PLAN SHOWING SHELF

TOP
MOULDING

0   1   2 FEET

AN OPEN DRESSER

Plate XIX

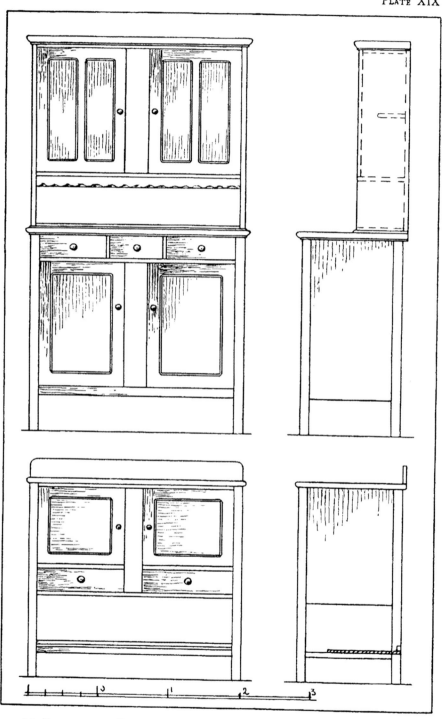

(1) Dresser with Doors to Top Shelves   (2) Dresser without Shelves

PLATE XX

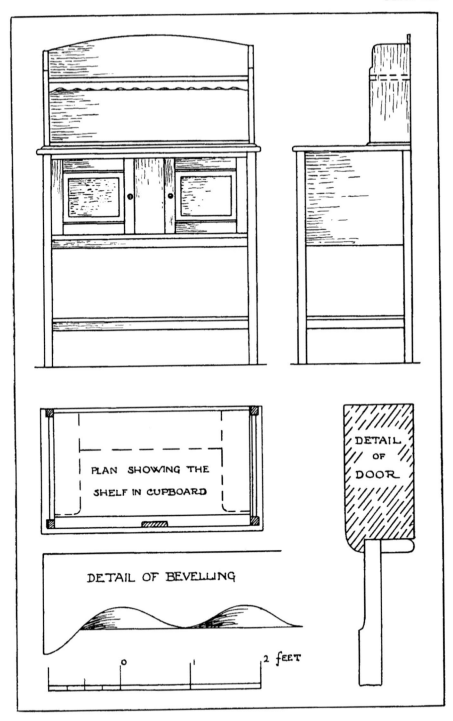

PLAN SHOWING THE
SHELF IN CUPBOARD

DETAIL
OF
DOOR

DETAIL OF BEVELLING

0   1   2 FEET

A SMALL DRESSER

Plate XXI

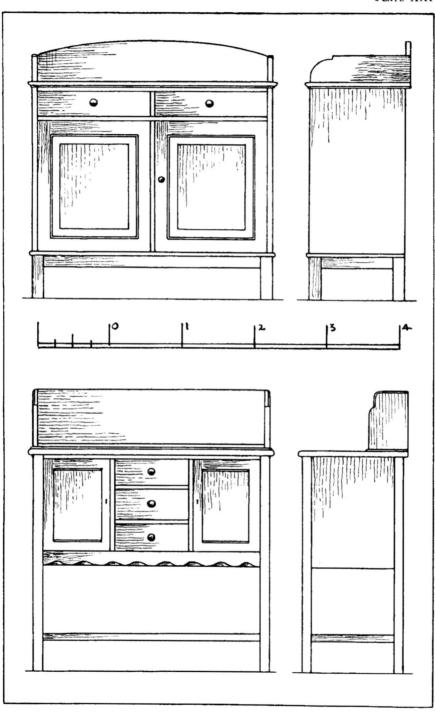

SMALL DRESSERS

PLATE XXII

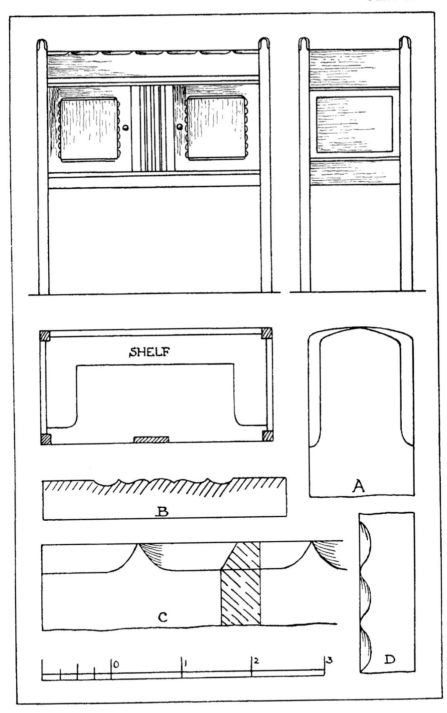

SHELF

A

B

C

D

0 1 2 3

AN OAK SIDEBOARD

Plate XXIII

A Mahogany Sideboard

IV. CHAIRS.

The Windsor and Stick Back Chairs—Stuff-over and Loose Seats. Wooden Seats
and Loose Cushions. The Settee, the Couch, and the Settle. Easy Chairs.

IN the tens of thousands of cottages and small houses which go to make
up the streets of our towns and cities, perhaps the most unsatisfactory
article of modern furniture is the chair. The only good examples are
copies of old ones, such as the Windsor, stick or ladder-back types, but
as these all have the kitchen stamp about them people look for a chair
which is a little more showy and find one in the plush seat stuffed with
anything but hair, a little bad carving on the back, and still worse
polishing or varnishing on the legs. The old Windsor chair with its
turned legs, many slats, and curved back is not so popular now there
is a demand for furniture which is easier to dust. In this respect one
can sympathise with the housewife, for probably no chair that is made
has so many parts and details as this well-known Windsor type. The
designs in this chapter are an attempt to strike a medium between the
flashy and flimsy modern chair and those which are generally associated
with the kitchen. It is claimed for these designs that they show chairs
which are strong, comfortable, and easy to clean. It is also hoped that
they are pleasant to look at. They can be made in any hard wood of
which oak, elm, beech, or birch are the most suitable. Those in the
photograph, Plate XXIV, are made in birch, stained a light brown. The
seat is concave and consists of a piece of thin $\frac{3}{8}$-in. birch pinned
down to the frame. A loose cushion which is strapped to the back legs
adds comfort to the seat. The backs are varied in design either with thin
slats or a wide splat. The legs are pinned into the projecting top rail, but
this is only one form, and an old one, of fixing the rail. Other designs
show the rail tenoned or dowelled into the legs. On Plate XXVIII
are five alternative designs and some details. A is a moulding run

(19)   5

down the edge of the second chair at the top and the last one at the bottom. A large detail of the front leg is shown with slightly rounded corners. In the photograph of the small oak sideboard (Plate XVI) there is a chair with a wide splat slightly pierced, and in the same plate there is a mahogany chair with a stuffed loose seat. Two other simple designs are shown with the kitchen table in Plate V, and they are best suited to a bedroom.

Arm-chairs are illustrated on Plate XXIX. The lower one C is one of two specially designed for an old couple, and are intended for warmth and a protection from draughts. The back is one panel of thin birch which will easily bend to the required curve. The sides are also panelled in. Legs and arms are rounded as seen in the detail of the top rail and panel at the head of the page. In Plate XXV there is a similar design of a heavier type.

A very simple arrangement for an adjustable back to an inexpensive easy chair is given on Plate XXX. The whole frame is made of 2-in. oak or any suitable hard wood. A shows the back in elevation and B the seat in plan. The slats are screwed flush into the frame and are intended to take thick loose cushions. In this design the usual method of providing a movable rod to support the back has been abandoned for a much simpler one. Slots are cut in the side rails as shown at C and D. The back drops into these slots and rests against the fixed back rail as seen in the section at D. To allow for the slots the side rails must be a $\frac{1}{2}$-in. wider than the front : and they must also be a $\frac{1}{2}$-in. thicker on the inside, although this can be avoided if the bottom rail of the back projects beyond the frame as the photograph shows in Plate XXVI. A piece of cane inserted at each side of the cushion will stiffen it and prevent it sagging when projecting over the front. The chair is strong, comfortable, and easy to keep clean. The cushions should be sewn together and the back one looped over the top. When the cushions are reversed the chair makes a day bed, E, for a child. Plate XXVI gives a view of the chair complete.

On Plate XXVII there is a small settee A, which would be suitable for the parlour in the newly designed cottages. It is 4 ft. 6 ins. long and has the usual drop end. A squab, or loose cushion on a webbed or wood slat base, and a simple line of stuffing round the ends and back should be all that is necessary for comfort and cleanliness.

The couch below, B, is much simpler in form. The upright head is built out to give a suitable slope for reclining and a cushion. The cost for such a couch is reduced to a minimum.

To people who like the old type of " settle " with a high back, the design at C is a suggestion for a small one. The seat which is slightly sloped is tenoned through the ends and the back is made up of two rails dovetailed into the back edges and filled in with vee-jointed matched boards. The edges where the arm would rest should be rounded. The sizes and the shape of the ends were taken from an old settle in a Somersetshire cottage. It was made of deal and had been painted a pleasant green. In Plate LIV there is a child's high chair and an arm-chair, both made in mahogany. They were part of a set for a living room in which the sideboard and small chair in Plate XVI were included, together with the corner china cabinet in Plate XXVI. An arm-chair, with what furniture people would call "a little more style" in it, is illustrated in Plate XXV. The front legs are distinctly Sheraton in form, but the back would not conform to that master craftsman's idea of delicate framing. In this case the intention was to design a strong well-shaped arm or " carving " chair for the dining-room.

What would be termed a " Hall seat " is shown in Plate XXIV, but as a matter of fact it is used for exactly the same purpose as a chesterfield in a living room, that is, with cushions as a comfortable seat, settle-wise, to draw up to the fire and screen off the door. Neither this seat nor the mahogany chair just described would be classed as " cheap " furniture, although middle-class people pay more for things not half as good. Both these examples are given to prove that good form and construction are first essentials to look for in furniture and not the meretricious ornament for which people blindly pay high prices. The simple strap carving on the Hall seat is just right and fit for its purpose and place, but if the panels had been carved the seat would then have been decorated for show and not made for use. In a similar way the back of the chair was made to rest against comfortably. That was the chief aim of the designer, whilst the front legs, though strong, could be more ornamental. It will be a fine day for craftsmanship when the British public realise some of these simple but essential principles, and are as willing to pay for their sound application to furniture as they now pay for embellishments which are neither right in practice or principle.

PLATE XXIV

CHAIRS WITH WOODEN SEATS AND LOOSE CUSHIONS

AN OAK SEAT

PLATE XXV

AN ARM-CHAIR WITH PANELLED BACK

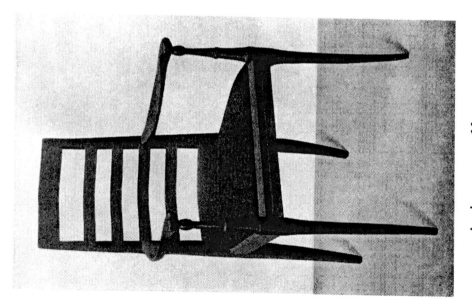

AN ARM-CHAIR IN MAHOGANY

PLATE XXVI

An Adjustable Easy Chair and China Shelves

PLATE XXVII

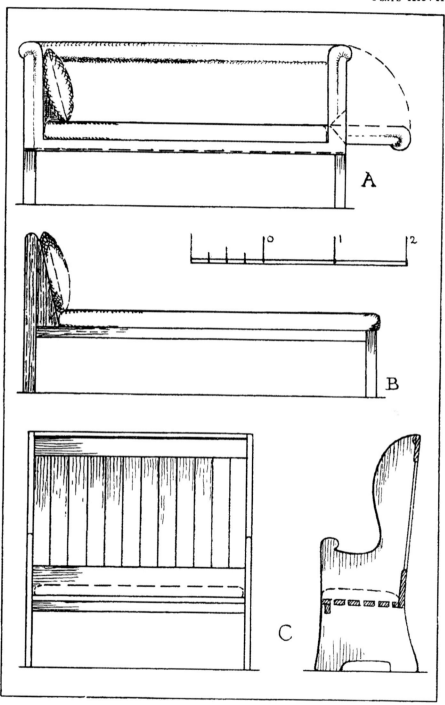

A. A SMALL CHESTERFIELD   B. A COUCH   C. A SETTLE

PLATE XXVIII

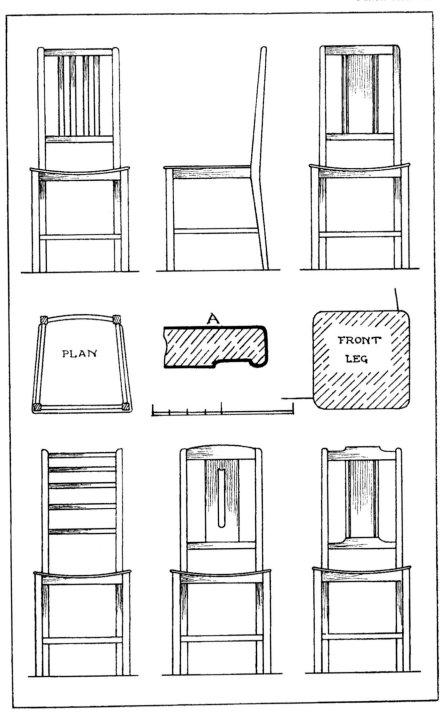

PLAN A FRONT LEG

DESIGNS FOR CHAIRS

PLATE XXIX

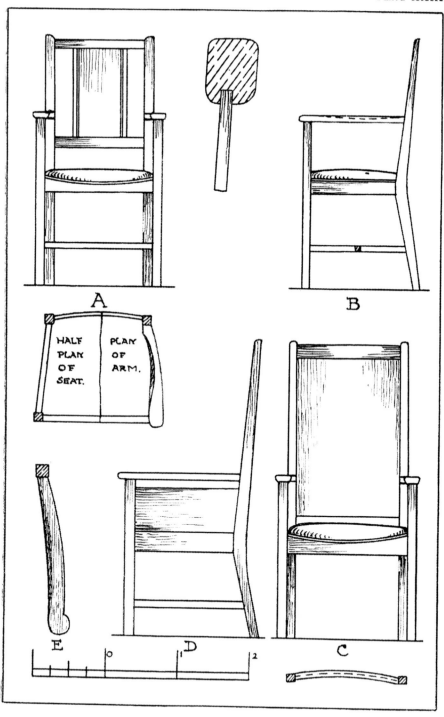

A

HALF
PLAN
OF
SEAT.

PLAN
OF
ARM.

E

D

C

B

DESIGNS FOR ARM-CHAIRS

PLATE XXX

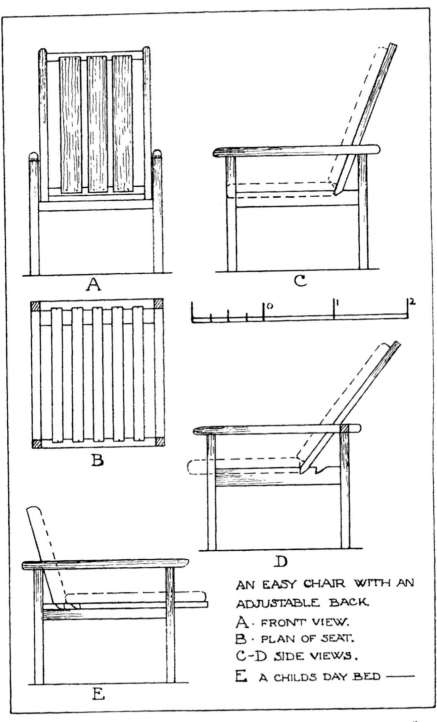

A

B

C

D

0   1   2

AN EASY CHAIR WITH AN
ADJUSTABLE BACK.
A. FRONT VIEW.
B. PLAN OF SEAT.
C-D SIDE VIEWS.
E A CHILDS DAY BED ——

E

V. BEDROOM FURNITURE.

Bedsteads—Wardrobes—Washstands—Combing.

In Plate I there is a general view of a complete set of bedroom furniture for what might be termed the "best," or largest bedroom, in a small house. The revival of wooden bedsteads is not only popular, but it is likely to develop into a permanent demand. The one seen in the photograph is a small "full size," but the drawing on Plate XLV gives similar designs for a full double and a single bed, namely, 4 ft. 6 ins., 3 ft., or 2 ft. 6 ins. The design for the head could be followed for either width. Details for the finish to the post, and a section of the framing are also shown. The designs are suitable for any hard wood, but the set in Plate I was made chiefly in birch and finished with wax polish. On Plate XL are designs for two small bedsteads, A and B, which were made in deal or whitewood and painted. The bed is shown in Plate III.

In designing the wardrobe the chief ideas were to combine strength with lightness, to discard unnecessary features, such as plinth and cornice, and yet to retain its right use as a wardrobe. It is 3 ft. wide and 6 ft. high, which leaves the usual inside dimensions for hanging purposes. On Plate XLIV is a scale drawing with details and a photograph is shown in Plate XXXI. The whole carcase is framed up and the panels are of three-ply wood. A method for a movable rod and hooks is illustrated in the wardrobe on Plate XLII. If a mirror is desired the glass should be fixed inside the door. The wardrobe on Plate XLII is just under 3 ft. wide and a drawer has been added. A detail shows how the glass can be fixed on the inside.

On Plate XLIII are designs for wardrobes 2 ft. 6 ins. wide. The one on the left was made in deal and whitewood, and is seen in the painted set in Plate III. The sectional plan shows the construction. The two wide uprights and the framed-up back are tongued, screwed, or nailed on to the ends which are solid, although they could be framed up. The top is dovetailed through and the moulding covers the dovetails. The door is "ledge and brace" with matched boarding, of which sections are shown in A and B. The rounded joint in B is perhaps the best. It should be clearly understood that this form of construction is suitable only for painted work in soft woods. Plate XXXII shows the wardrobe painted. The wardrobe on the right of Plate XLIII is framed up and could be made in any wood.

Fig. 7 illustrates a strong method of button fastening for the doors.

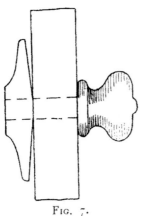

FIG. 7.
A Button Fastening.

The pin from the knob runs through the button, and a metal pin keeps the button fixed.

On Plate XLI are drawings for a corner wardrobe with two doors. The construction is quite simple. The framed-up backs are screwed together at the angle and again into the uprights. Top and bottom may also be screwed, and the whole thing can be easily taken apart for removal.

Plate XXXIII shows a painted matched door wardrobe with double doors. The combing on the boards is distinctly seen and a similar pattern is enlarged in Fig. 9. The construction of this wardrobe is given in detail on Plate XXIX. The front is composed of a frame, mortised and tenoned together. The back is also framed, but is of course panelled. These two frames are fixed flush to the skeleton carcase and they also form the feet. The whole structure is kept rigid by these frames, and they can be applied to solid or panelled ends.

There are two designs on Plate XXXVIII for small wardrobes reduced to the minimum in width which is about 2 ft. 3 ins. The one on the left is made in a similar way to the description given above. On the right a curtain is used in place of doors.

Washstands.—Assuming that every new house to be built will be provided with a bathroom and basin, the washstand must still remain a necessary piece of furniture in the bedroom. One bathroom could not provide washing accommodation for every member of the family, and

there are times which come to every household when the washstand in
the bedroom is essential.

In Plate XXXIV a very simple and cheap stand is shown.   It has

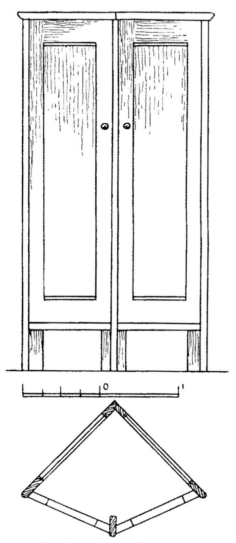

Fig. 8.—A Corner Cupboard.

curtains in place of doors and a splash curtain at the back.   A drawing
of the same stand is given on Plate XXXVII.   The front line of the
top is curved which gives a little wider space.   The top itself is covered
with lino, and a detail, C, shows the rim rebated to take it.   The rim

should be dry dowelled into the top so that it can be lifted off and the lino cleaned right through. The front line of the lino is protected by a small bead pinned down as shown in the detail B. Two posts for the curtain are halved over the rim and screwed from behind.

Plate XXXIII and the top drawing on Plate XXXVII show an even cheaper type of construction for a painted washstand. Front and

FIG. 9.—A "Combed" Pattern.

back frames are fixed to the ends, A, and the bottom, but the back frame is carried up to form a splash board. Two doors are made from matched boarding.

In the belief that corner washstands are not so unpopular as they are said to be, the author has designed two. One is shown with a chest of drawers in Plate XXXV. It is made of $\frac{3}{4}$-in. wood through-out and curtains would enclose the lower part. The plan and details are given on Plate XXXVI together with a design on the left which contains a little more work. The back is framed up and panels or curtains could be used to protect the wall from splashes. Curtains are also used in the lower part. Below the corner washstands is a medicine cupboard with two doors. The construction is very simple. A shows the top screwed into the uprights. In Plate XXXIV there is a very small washstand with a tambour or shutter front which should be cheaper than two panelled doors. The little table with it is for use at the bedside.

In Fig. 8 a corner cupboard is shown which would be useful anywhere, in living room, bedroom, or kitchen. It is just under 5 ft. high, and the front has been brought out to prevent any tipping. The plan shows the two framed backs, the front edges of which are rounded. The bottom is screwed through the frames and the top also screwed down into them. By this means the whole thing could be easily taken to pieces if required.

Combing.—In Plate XLVI there are nine suggestions for combing patterns in paint. Black on a coloured ground is given as being more suited for reproduction, but any two colours which blend well can be used. The comb, which is made in varying thicknesses of spurs, or teeth, must be used freely, consequently the scrolled and wavy patterns are the most successful. They are best, too, for getting round the corners. Suggestions for panelling out are given at the bottom of the page. In the process there will be numerous accidentals which give a livelier interest to the pattern as when lines are crossed, and it looks as though the comb had been raised and the pattern jumped at the intersection. With practice the combing can be done very quickly.

Fig. 9 is produced by kind permission of the editor of *The Builder*.

PLATE XXXI

A WARDROBE

PLATE XXXII

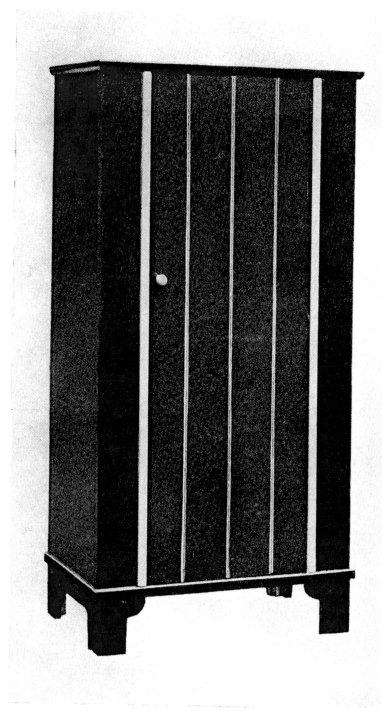

A DEAL WARDROBE, PAINTED

PLATE XXXIII

A WARDROBE AND WASHSTAND, PAINTED

Plate XXXIV

A Dressing Chest and Washstand, Painted

Washstand and Bedside Table

Plate XXXV

Corner Washstand, Dressing Chest, and Chair, Painted

PLATE XXXVI

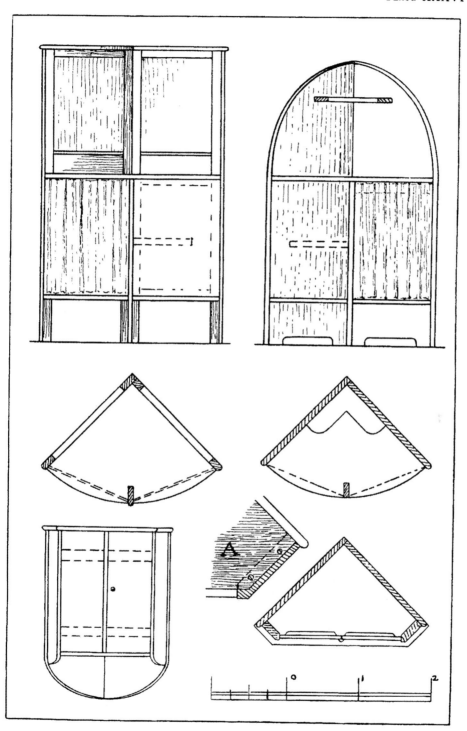

CORNER WASHSTANDS AND CUPBOARDS

Plate XXXVII

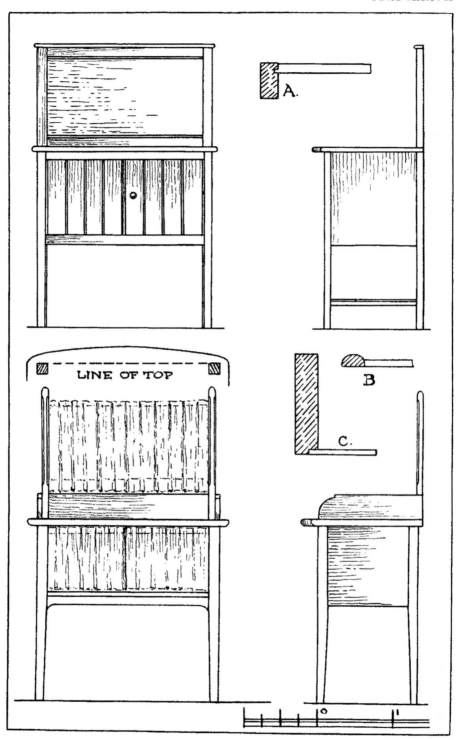

LINE OF TOP

A.

B

C.

Washstands

PLATE XXXVIII

SMALL WARDROBES

Plate XXXIX

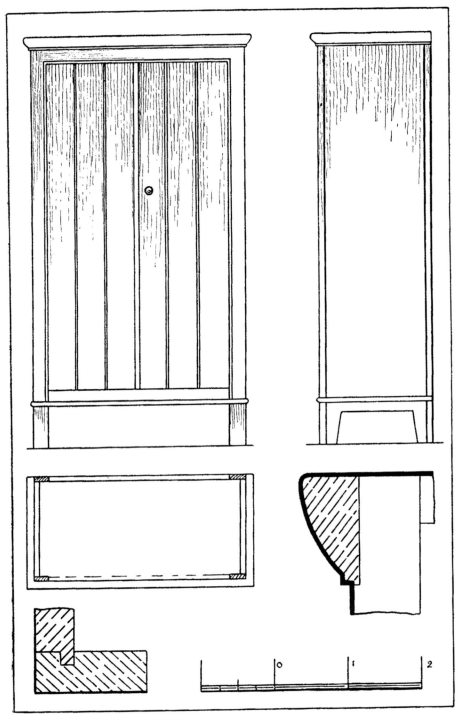

A Wardrobe

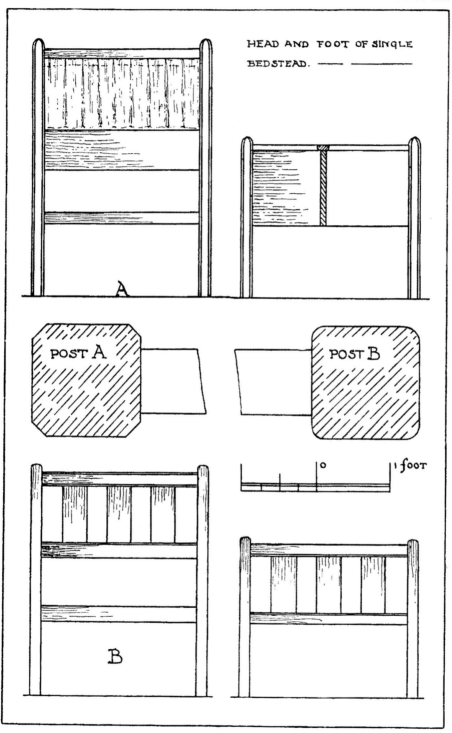

Plate XL

HEAD AND FOOT OF SINGLE BEDSTEAD.

A

POST A

POST B

0   1 foot

B

PLATE XLI

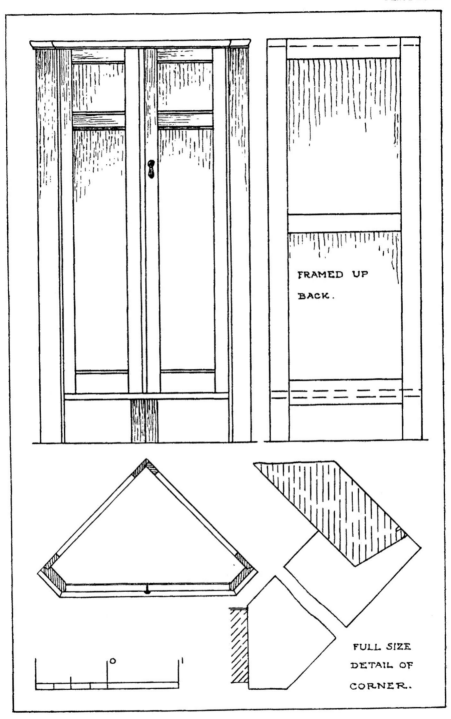

FRAMED UP
BACK.

FULL SIZE
DETAIL OF
CORNER.

A CORNER WARDROBE

PLATE XLII

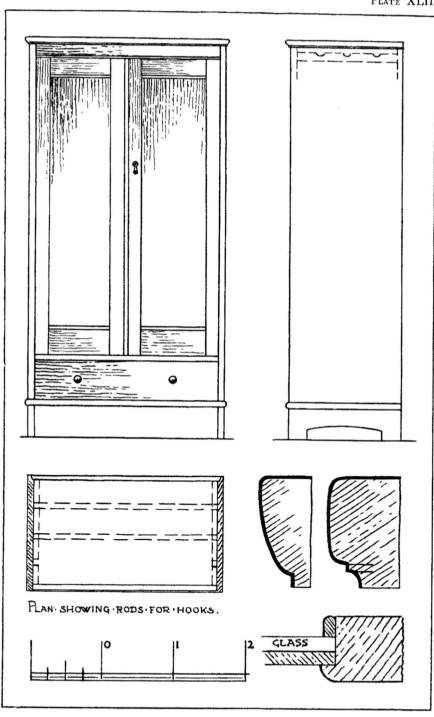

PLAN·SHOWING·RODS·FOR·HOOKS.

GLASS

A Wardrobe with Drawer

Plate XLIII

Plate XLIV

SECTION OF RAIL

DETAIL OF POST

A "Framed-up" Wardrobe

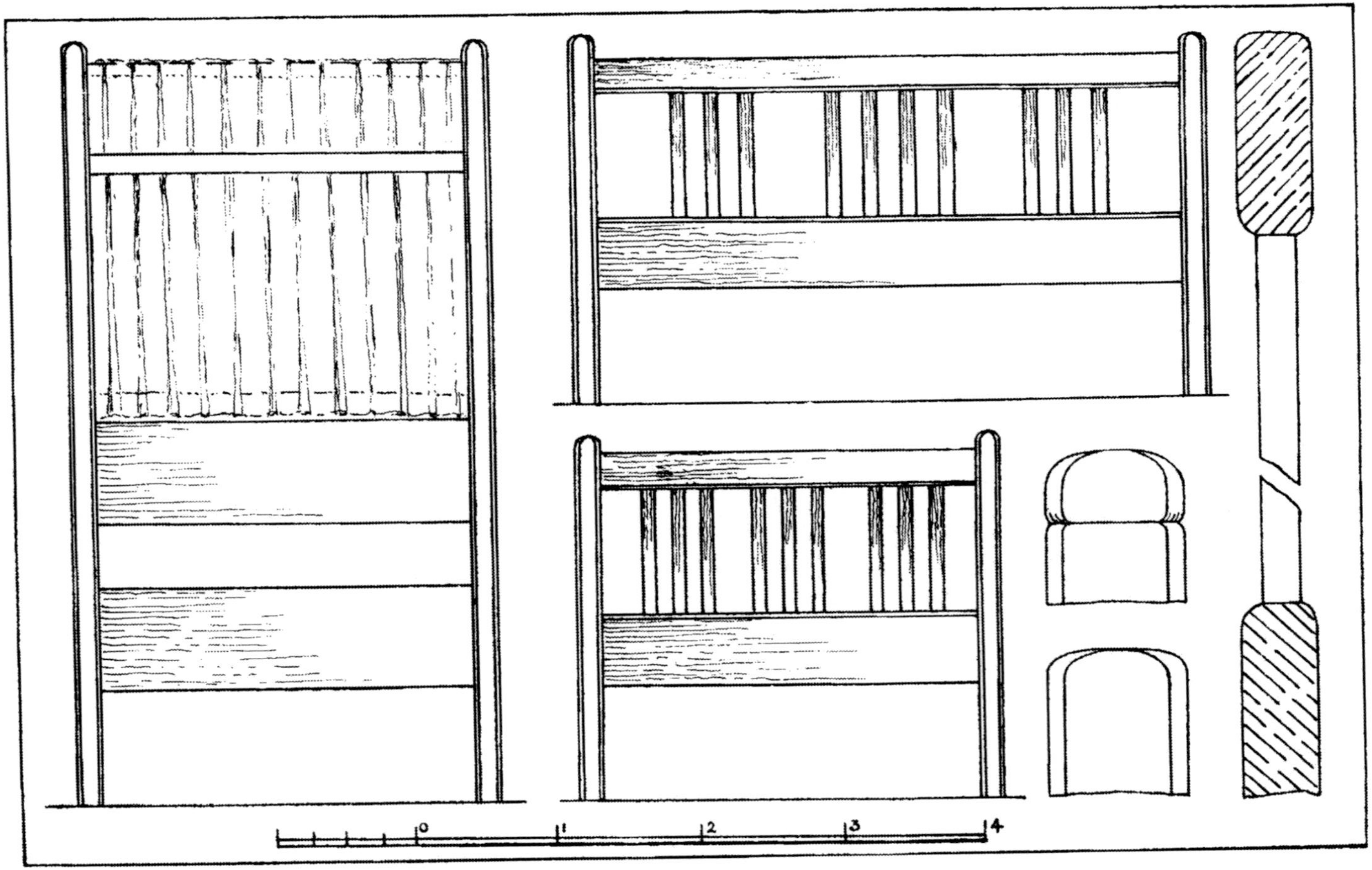

Plate XLV

Bedsteads

PLATE XLVI

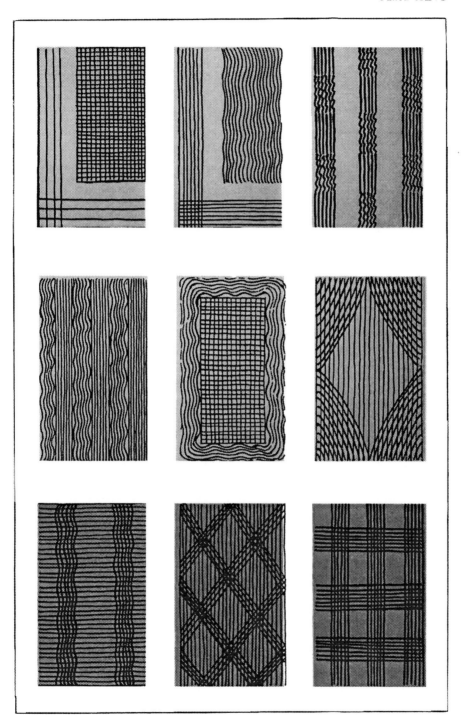

PATTERNS FOR COMBING

VI. BEDROOM FURNITURE (*Continued*).

Chests of Drawers—Toilet Mirrors—Towel Horses and Rails.

THE modern chest of drawers is either very good or extremely bad. The best examples are those of the eighteenth-century type which stood well up from the floor. Very little good can be said for the cheaper chests which are grained to look like oak, maple, or mahogany, and when they stand flat to the floor they are an assured dust trap, for being heavy they are seldom moved.

The chest in the best set is shown in Plate XLVII. It has a hat cupboard at the top in which there is a sliding rack or shelf for hats or light things. No such provision for hats is made in wardrobes or bedroom furniture, and the general verdict on this cupboard has been one of cordial approval. If made a little higher a third drawer could be added if desired. In the drawing, Plate L, there is a book rack on the top.

The dressing chest at the top of Plate L is 2 ft. 9 ins. long. It is made like the painted wardrobe and is consequently very strong and rigid, the two frames on the cut-out ends forming the feet. A smaller chest is shown in Plate XXXIV with the washstand. Both chests were painted and the combing can be clearly seen.

Every one knows the usual type of mahogany mirror with its scroll supports and its " serpentine " base. It has been the accepted design for a hundred years. Every one knows, too, how the supports work loose and the screws wear out so that the glass must be tied to its proper angle or propped up with a book. On Plate XXXV the glass swings from the top and is supported by a wood strut, a method which is clearly illustrated in the photograph where the frame is fixed to the chest. In Plate XXXIV the mirror is movable and the design is suggested as an alternative to the aforesaid " serpentine " and " scroll " glass. It is simpler in construction, can be made in any wood, and should be cheaper to produce. On Plate LII there is a scale drawing with details of the post and slot at A and of the post forked into the tray side at B. The second design shows the glass supported in slots cut into the tray side. The detail C gives the slots cut in the back for the strut. This second design would be a little cheaper than the first, whilst the third one D at the bottom is just the mirror frame screwed at an angle to brackets. The screws pass through the frame from inside the rebate. This makes quite a strong and serviceable little mirror. All three have been made and answer their purpose satisfactorily.

In Plate XLVII a simply made towel horse is shown with the chest of drawers. The shelf at the bottom might be useful for shoes. On Plate XLIX there are useful designs for towel rails which can be fixed on the ends of washstands or on the wall. They are made up of arms which swing from a centre in a bracket. In the top one, A, the arms are

Fig. 10.—Towel Rail for Bathroom.

pinned right through, and if a knob is turned on the top of the pin it will keep its place without any further fixture. The arms should be of hard wood, birch, or sycamore for preference. They need not be more than $\frac{3}{4}$-in. thick, and four, or more, would swing from one pin. The second, B, is confined to two arms which swing on separate pins. Half-inch wood should be quite thick enough for all the parts. The third, C, is a suggestion for one arm only, and the top pin fits into a piece which is slot screwed and can be pushed up and down to release or fix the arm. At the bottom of the page are suggestions for the more ordinary type of towel horse. Fig. 10 is a simple arrangement for a towel rail suitable for a bathroom. The rails are the usual $\frac{3}{8}$-in. or $\frac{1}{2}$-in. beech dowels bored into brackets one above the other as shown in the end. The back board is easily fixed to the wall or woodwork.

Designs for two dressing tables are given on Plate LI. The usual method of swinging the glass from the centre has been abandoned in both designs. A wooden dowel in the frame is dropped into a slot cut in the side supports at the top. The glass is held at convenient slopes by a small wooden strut which in the top table is hinged to the glass frame, and small slots are cut in the base board to act as the rack, see Plate XLVIII. In the bottom table the strut is hinged on to the back board and works in slots cut into the back of the mirror frame. These simple devices are inexpensive and reliable. There is never any fear of the glass turning somersault when the screws wear out. Wooden knobs are suggested for the drawers. In the lower design there is a shelf for shoes. This of course adds a little to the cost, but the table could be made without the shelf if desired.

In some of the designs the top projects at the back to clear the skirting, but in the dressing tables the top has been left flush, as such tables are generally placed back to the window and a short distance from it.

Plate XLVII

Towel Horse and Chest of Drawers, with Cupboard

Plate XLVIII

A Chair and Toilet Table

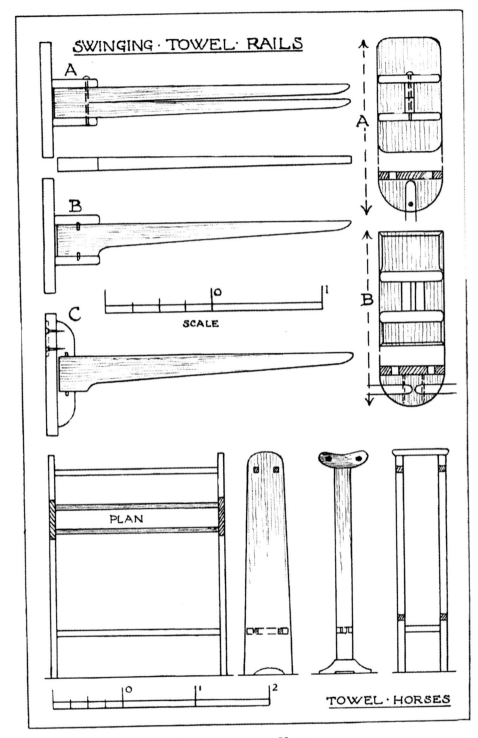

Plate XLIX

SWINGING · TOWEL · RAILS

A

B

C

A

B

SCALE

0 1

PLAN

TOWEL · HORSES

0 1 2

Towel Rails and Horses

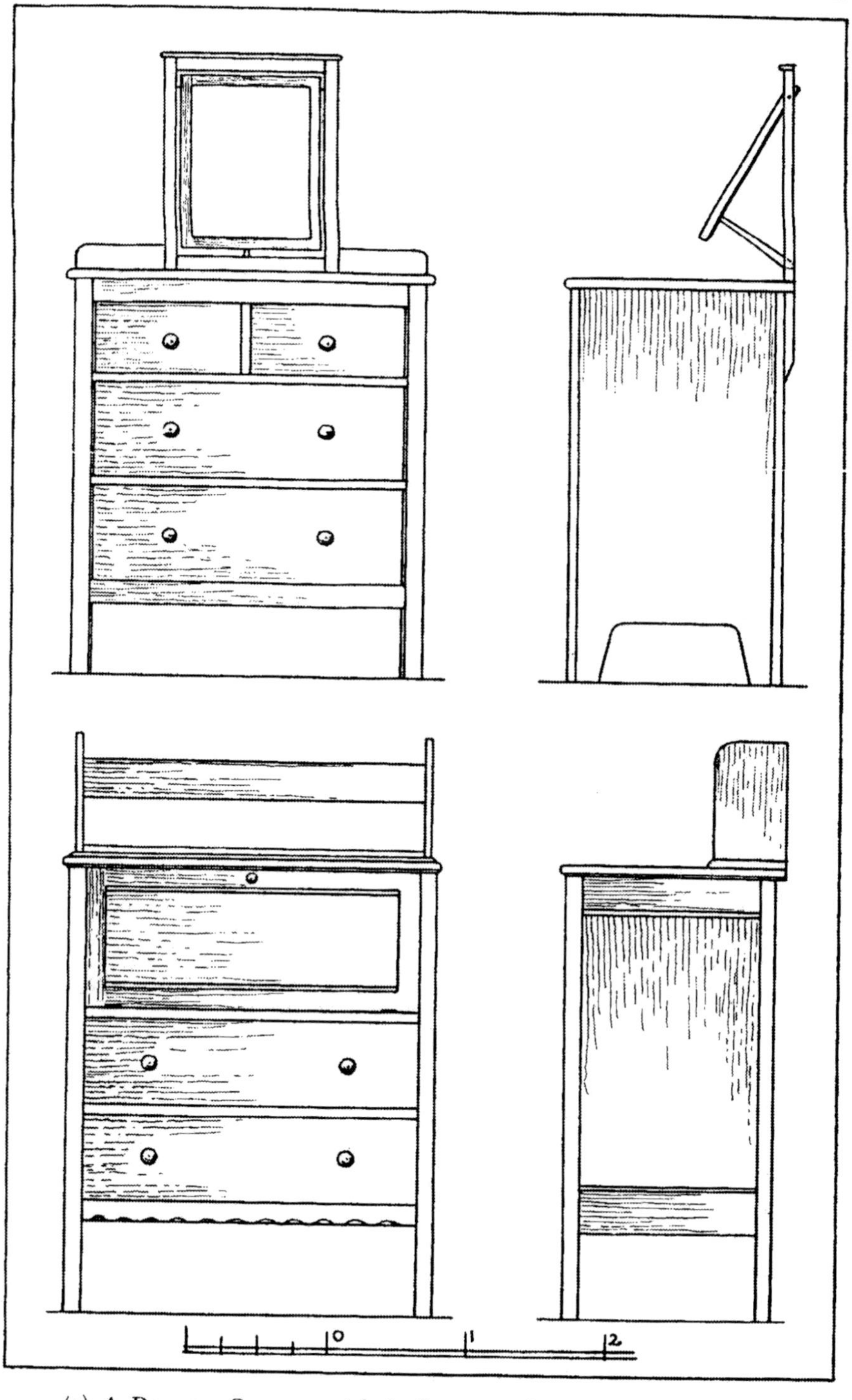

PLATE L

(1) A Dressing Chest   (2) A Cupboard Chest with Book Shelf

Plate LI

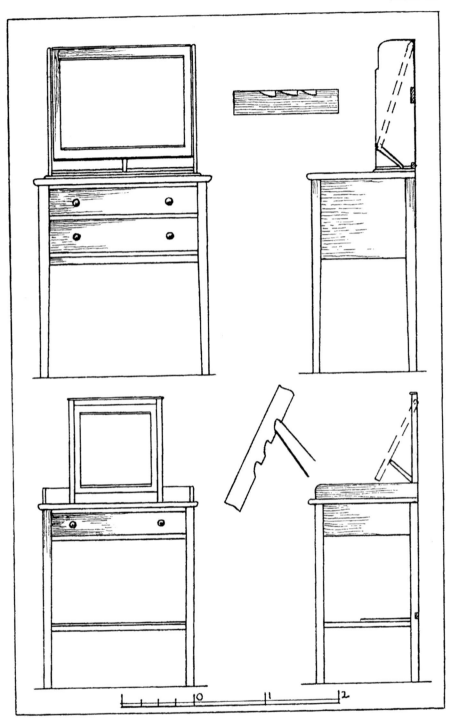

TOILET TABLES

PLATE LII

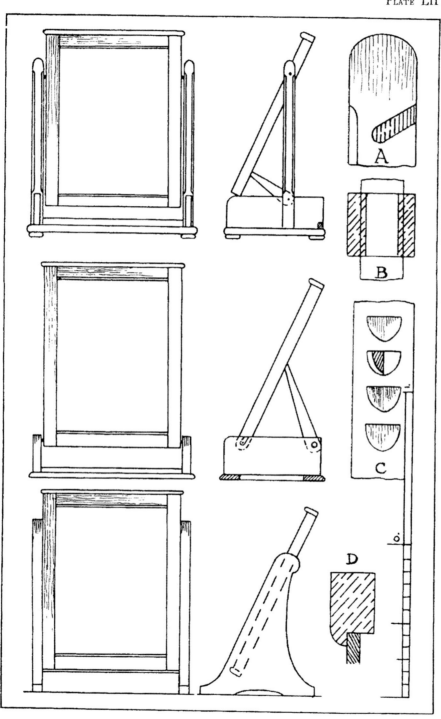

DESIGN FOR TOILET MIRROR FRAMES

VII. MISCELLANEOUS FURNITURE.

Bookcases—China Cabinets—Hat Stands—Whatnots.

THE bookcase and cupboard illustrated in Plate XV and drawn to scale on Plate LVI would be a useful piece of furniture in the living room or the parlour. It would fit a recess or stand-out in the room. There are no special features about it, except perhaps the chamfered edges of the ends and on the dividing piece in the centre of the upper part. These chamfers or bevels give a little more character to the design and allow the shelves to set back from the edge. The cupboard would be useful for storing magazines which always look untidy when left about the room. Where such a bookcase is not possible, the book and paper rack on the same page should make a very good substitute. Papers and periodicals of all sorts quickly accumulate, and such a rack will hold a good number. Both the case and the rack could be made in any wood, hard or soft.

The old-fashioned, and still popular, but usually ugly "whatnot" fills an odd corner in a room and provides a place for the odd things which "willy nilly" have to be kept somewhere. In Plate XXVI a useful tier of shelves is shown in the corner of the small parlour, and on Plate LV there is a scale drawing of the same article. The construction differs from the ordinary "whatnot" with its turned or twisted supports just pinned into the thin shelves. The elevation, A, shows two frames tenoned together without panels and securely screwed at the angle. The front stiles or uprights are made wide enough to be cut out for the smallest shelf at the top. The shelves are screwed through the frame from the back and a centre leg is fixed under the bottom shelf. B is the section showing full shape of one frame. C is a similar set of shelves with a cupboard at the bottom. The construction is the same as the first except that panels would be grooved in the back where the

(33)

cupboards are. D is a set of shelves for hanging. The two back boards would be solid and the shelves just screwed through. E is a tier of book shelves for a corner. They can be made in a similar way to the "whatnot," and the frames or solid backs rebated into the uprights. There is no waste space in the corner if smaller books are arranged in a semicircle.

For corner china cupboards there are two designs on Plate LVII, the first one, A, with open shelves above and the second, B, with glass doors. Both these cabinets could be made in one carcase, but they are better made in two with the top screwed down to the bottom. The whole construction is very simple with framed-up backs rebated into uprights. Shaping for the shelves, for which suggestions are given, is a matter of choice as they could be kept their full width and level with the front.

In Plate LIV there is a mahogany china cabinet for a corner. The quarter circle front complicates the construction somewhat, but the doors are straight. The turned legs are forked up into the frieze frame.

A straight front china cabinet is also shown in Plate LIV. It was made in mahogany for which the design is best suited. The ends are glazed as well as the doors, but they could be solid if the cost had to be reduced. The dimensions are 5 ft. 6 ins. high, 2 ft. 9 ins. wide, and depth 10 ins. to 12 ins. outside.

It is safe to say that one of the ugliest and most ill-constructed pieces of household furniture is the hat-stand with a centre upright and tiers of curly arms on either side. It usually trembles when you hang a light coat on it and staggers under weight of a heavy one. The more modern stands are not much better although they are not so likely to collapse.

It is hoped that in the new houses some provision will be made in the way of cupboards, under stairs or in a recess, for the keeping of hats, coats, and umbrellas. They are not the best decoration for a hall at any time, and our villas have been built in such a way that the hall, or front passage, is the only possible place to put a hat-stand, which generally takes half or more of the floor space.

A recess with doors or a curtain in front is probably the best arrangement where possible. Failing a recess, a shallow skeleton cupboard about 5 ft. high with a curtain to pull across is very satisfactory. Old ideas are hard to kill, and it may take a long time to convince

Plate LIII

A Hat and Umbrella-Stand made in Oak

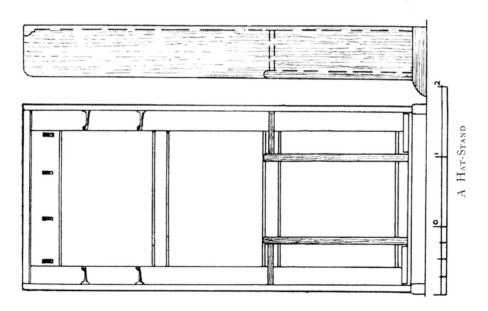

A Hat-Stand

people that the modern hat stand is unsightly and takes up more room than it need do. Plate LIII shows a suggestion for a stand which need not take more than 11 ins. at the base and 9 ins. for the end. It is just a framed-up back, open to the wall, screwed on to the solid ends into which a bottom board has been dovetailed. The design could be lengthened another 2 ft. if desired and the back panelled up. Plate LIII

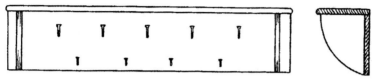

FIG. 11.—Coat and Hat Rack.

also shows a larger and more expensive stand panelled right through, but in depth it takes less room than the ordinary stand with a drawer, and in production it should not cost more. If a small shelf is required there is plenty of room for one in each angle above the umbrella rack. For a simple hanging arrangement, Fig. 11, shows a shelf with a back on which the hooks are fixed. The back board gives good fixing to the wall and the shelf would take hats.

PLATE LIV

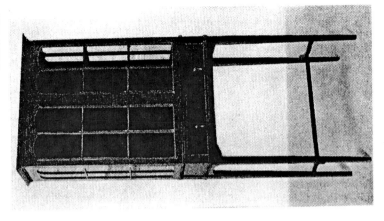

A China Cabinet in Mahogany

A Corner China Cabinet, Arm and Child's Chairs

PLATE LV

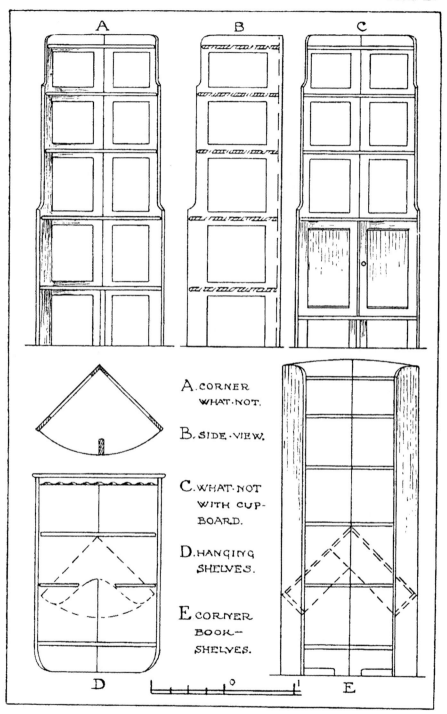

A. CORNER
WHAT·NOT.

B. SIDE·VIEW.

C. WHAT·NOT
WITH CUP-
BOARD.

D. HANGING
SHELVES.

E CORNER
BOOK—
SHELVES.

CORNER BOOK AND CHINA SHELVES

PLATE LVII

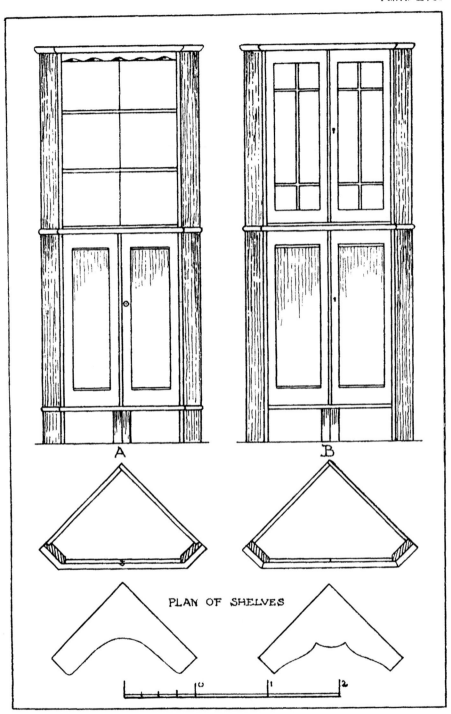

A   B

PLAN OF SHELVES

CORNER CHINA CABINETS

PLATE LVI

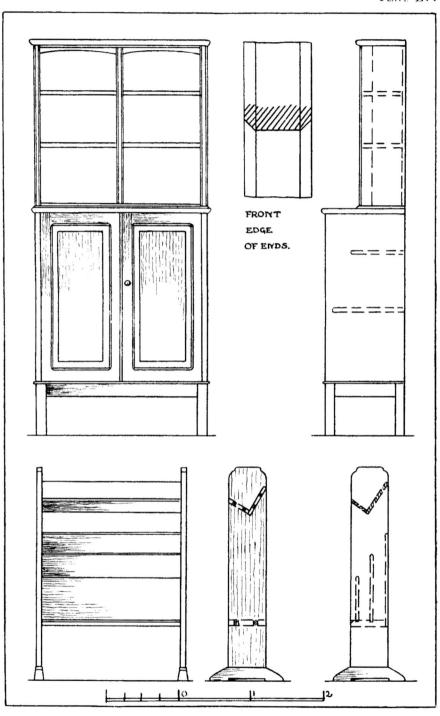

FRONT
EDGE
OF ENDS.

(1) A BOOKCASE AND CUPBOARD
(2) A BOOK AND PAPER RACK

10

CPSIA information can be obtained at www.ICGtesting.com
Printed in the USA
BVOW060506240413

318988BV00003B/183/A

9 781905 217489